BRAIN BOOSTERS

T0105424

NATURE PUZZLES

by
Vicky Barker
& Ste Johnson

Little GENIUS BOOKS

Published by Little Genius Books. www.littlegeniusbooks.com. • 10 9 8 7 6 5 4 3 2 1 • 9781953344434

Text and illustrations copyright © 2021 b small publishing ltd. Art Director: Vicky Barker. Editorial: Sam Hutchinson. Printed in China by WKT Co. Ltd.
All rights reserved. No reproduction, copy or transmission of this publication may be made without written permission. No part of this publication may be reproduced, stored in a retrieval system or transmitted in any form or by any means, electronic, mechanical, photocopying, recording or otherwise, without the prior permission of the publisher.

Add sad faces or happy faces to these fish.
Draw their scales and color them in.

Follow the turtle's path to find out where it is heading.
A
C
A
R
I
T
S
C
O

Carl eats only leaves with even answers.
Carly eats only the ones with odd answers.
Which caterpillar eats the most leaves?

Finish these patterns found in nature.
Can you think of any more?

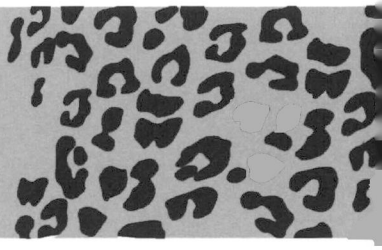

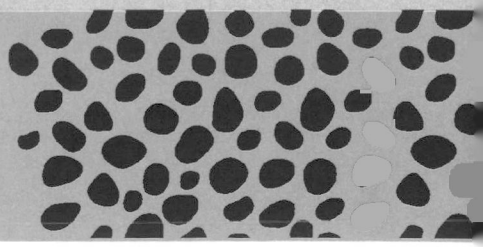

DID YOU KNOW? *Camouflage can help animals to hide from predators or to hunt for prey.*

Connect the dots to add some fishy friends to this coral reef.
Color in the beautiful scene.

Add symmetrical patterns to the shells of these baby sea turtles.

DID YOU KNOW?

Leatherback sea turtles have been known to dive over 3,000 feet (1,000 m) deep in the ocean.

Help this bee
get to the flower.
A
B
C

Coral reefs are full of dashing colors and stunning fish. Create your own colorful scene below.

DID YOU KNOW?

Coral reefs look like complicated rock structures, but they are actually made up of animals called corals and plants called algae.

Dive into this underwater word search.

F	Y	D	I	V	E	R	S	V	M	S	H	H	S	H	K
I	S	X	K	T	U	R	T	P	E	U	S	X	T	M	T
S	S	Q	S	P	E	C	I	E	S	I	L	U	U	A	R
D	T	O	U	W	R	H	M	K	F	D	H	S	R	X	O
H	A	L	R	I	Q	J	H	A	L	G	A	E	T	M	P
P	R	F	E	V	D	E	B	L	M	A	X	A	L	J	I
L	F	E	F	D	S	L	E	N	H	X	H	W	E	H	C
K	I	E	F	X	L	L	L	A	R	O	C	E	M	S	A
E	S	R	B	E	G	Y	X	P	O	C	X	E	V	H	L
Y	H	P	H	S	K	F	M	C	R	T	X	D	H	A	M
F	D	S	L	O	W	I	N	K	L	O	U	Q	W	R	A
B	U	B	B	L	E	S	X	D	X	P	V	X	U	K	R
Q	L	G	X	J	F	H	N	X	M	U	K	E	L	P	C
G	R	O	C	E	A	N	S	H	E	S	K	L	E	S	M
J	A	L	S	E	A	W	R	E	F	L	L	E	H	K	P
K	B	A	D	E	E	P	S	E	A	X	M	B	A	R	C

FISH	OCEAN	SHARK	JELLYFISH
CORAL	OCTOPUS	DEEP SEA	SEAWEED
REEF	DIVER	BUBBLES	SPECIES
KELP	STARFISH	ALGAE	SQUID
TROPICAL	TURTLE	SHELL	CRAB

Each of these rows of flowers has a different number pattern. Can you work out the pattern and fill in the blank spaces?

Find the odd one out in each row.

Match these deep-sea creatures to their shadows.

You are on safari! What can you see out of the window?

True or false?

1. In Svalbard, Norway, it is light from mid-April to mid-August with no night.

2. If a fish holds its breath long enough, it can float out of the water and start to fly.

3. The Sahara Desert is 3,000 miles (4,800 k) wide.

4. The largest ocean is the Indian Ocean.

5. There are around 12 times more trees on Earth than stars in the Milky Way galaxy.

6. Pineapples take a year to grow.

How many different animals have passed through here?

DID YOU KNOW?

Animal tracks can tell you what kind of animal made them, how large it was, when the tracks were made, and how fast the animal was traveling at that time.

Can you spot ten differences in these scenes?

DID YOU KNOW?

The word cephalopod comes from the Greek word for "head-feet." Common types of cephalopods include octopuses, squid, and cuttlefish.

Help this firefly find its way back to its friends.
START HERE

Use this step-by-step guide to draw a sleepy sloth.

Find the group of fish that matches the group on the right.

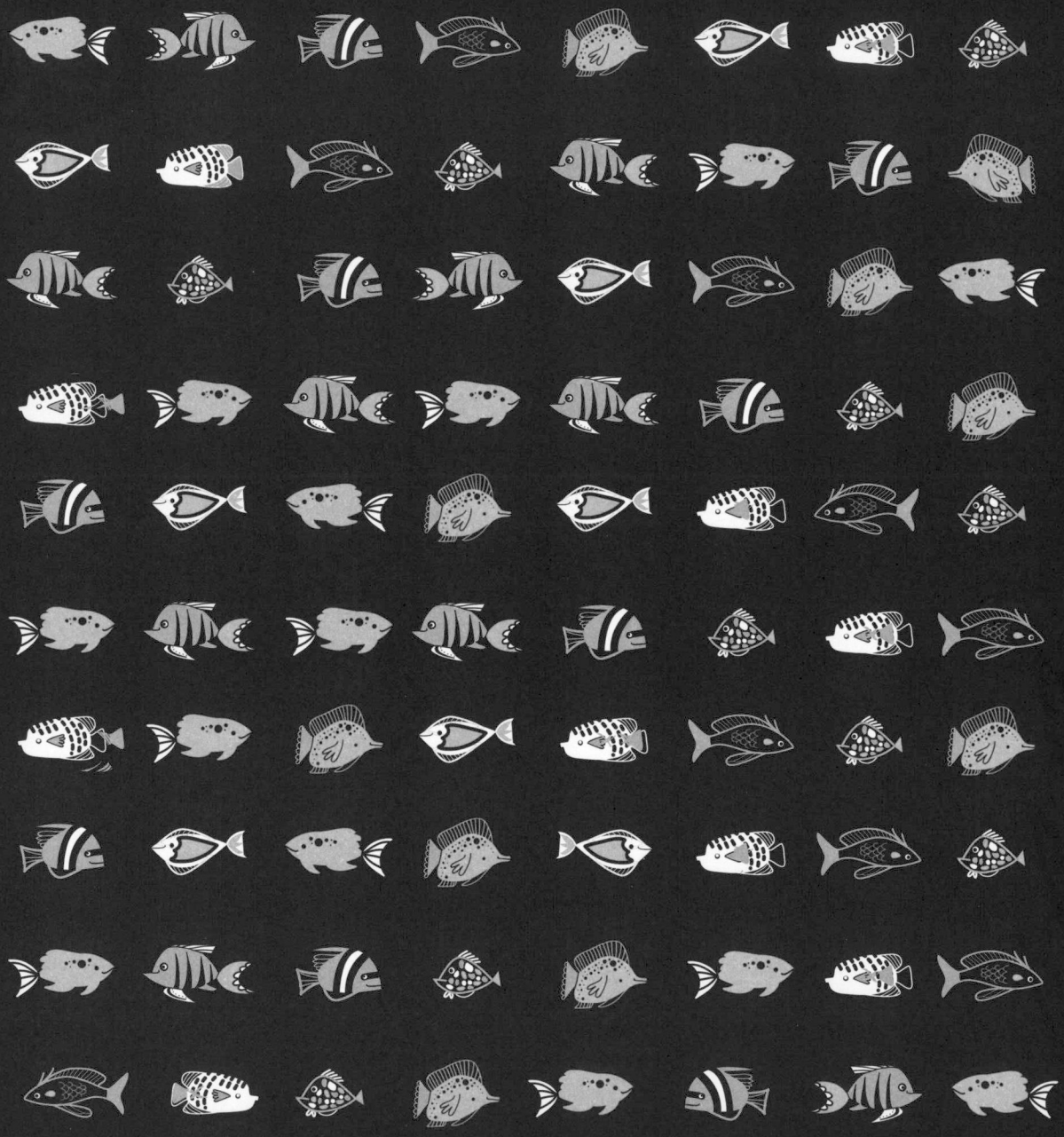

You have discovered a new species of insect in the depths of the rainforest! Draw what it looks like and give it a name.

DID YOU KNOW?

The Catacanthus incarnatus is also known as the "Man-faced stink bug!" The markings on its wings resemble a man's face!

Reunite this goat with its friend, and guide them both safely back up the mountain. Watch out for clouds and trees blocking your path.

Draw the rest of these butterflies and color them in.

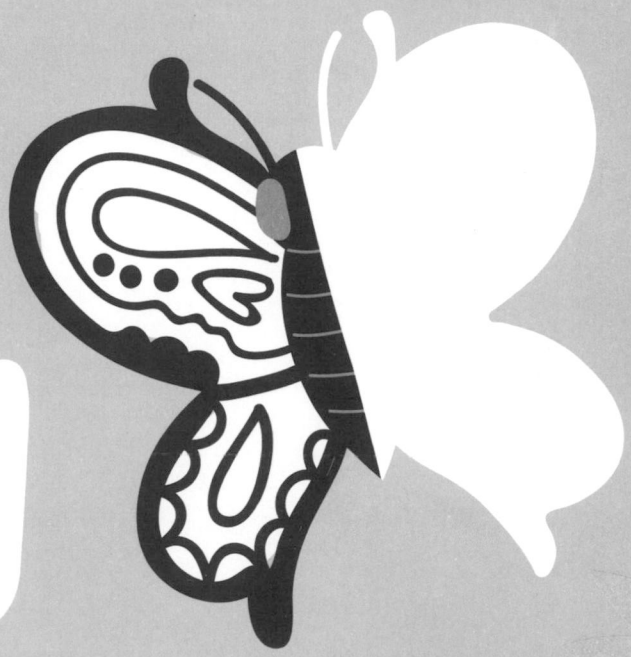

DID YOU KNOW?

Butterflies have transparent wings, and they taste with their feet.

How quickly can you get this baby shark back to its dad?
Draw a line as fast as you can without going off the path.
Time yourself!

Can you copy this toucan picture in the grid below?

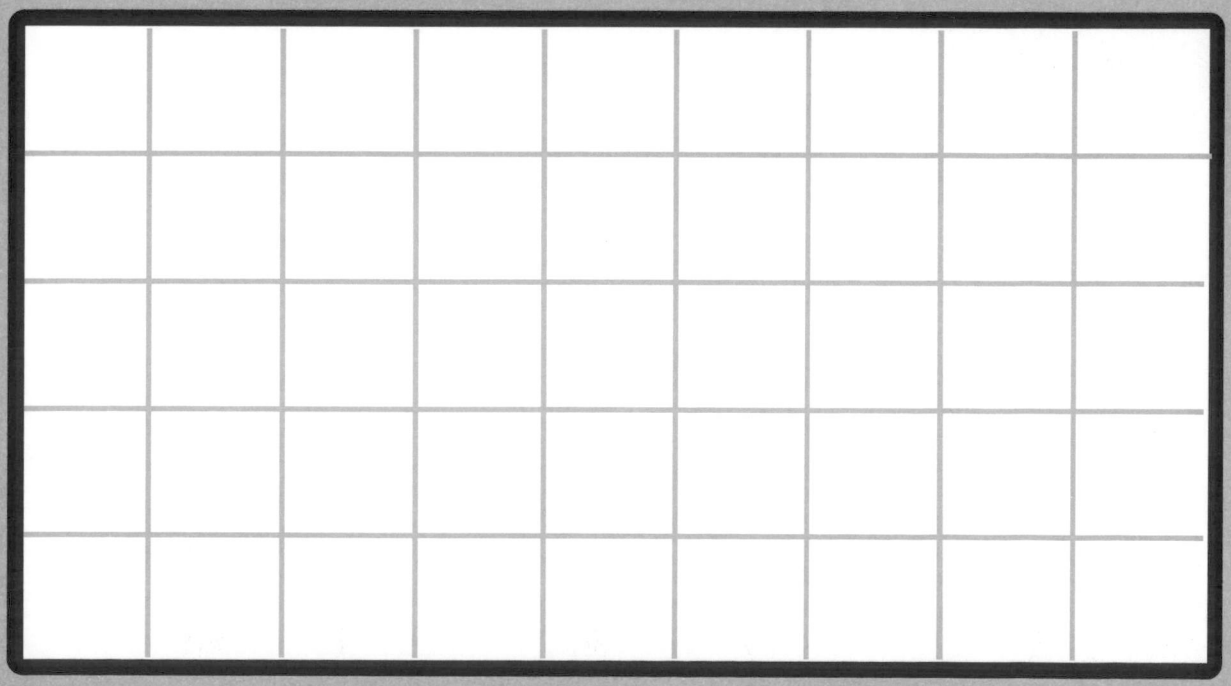

The sky is glowing! Can you make your way through the pretty Northern Lights maze?

Subtract all the spaces with a dot marked in them by coloring them in. You will reveal a picture with the spaces left behind!

Are these bees or ladybugs? You decide!

DID YOU KNOW?

To produce a pound of honey, bees fly the equivalent of three times around the world.

Can you work out the answers to these?

Add patterns to these shells.

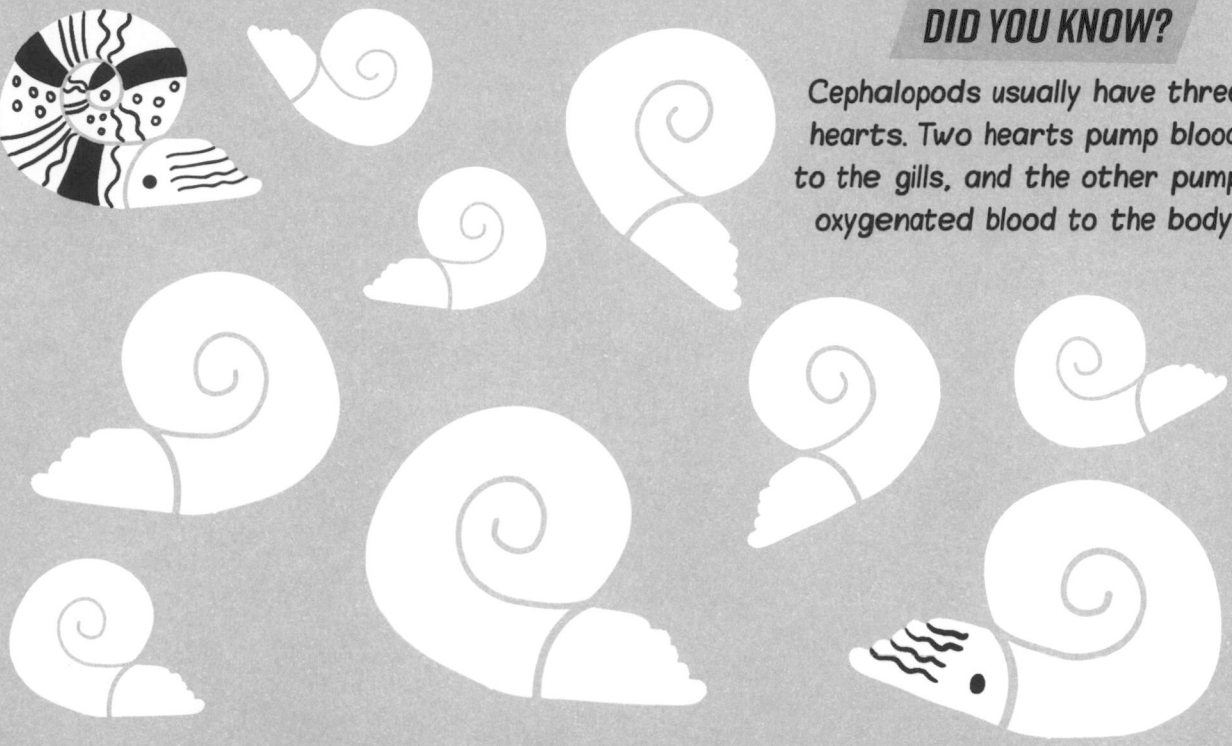

DID YOU KNOW?

Cephalopods usually have three hearts. Two hearts pump blood to the gills, and the other pumps oxygenated blood to the body.

One of these starfish is unique.
Can you spot which one?

DID YOU KNOW?

Starfish have no brain or blood. They use filtered sea water to pump nutrients through their nervous system.

Are there more fireflies or stars?

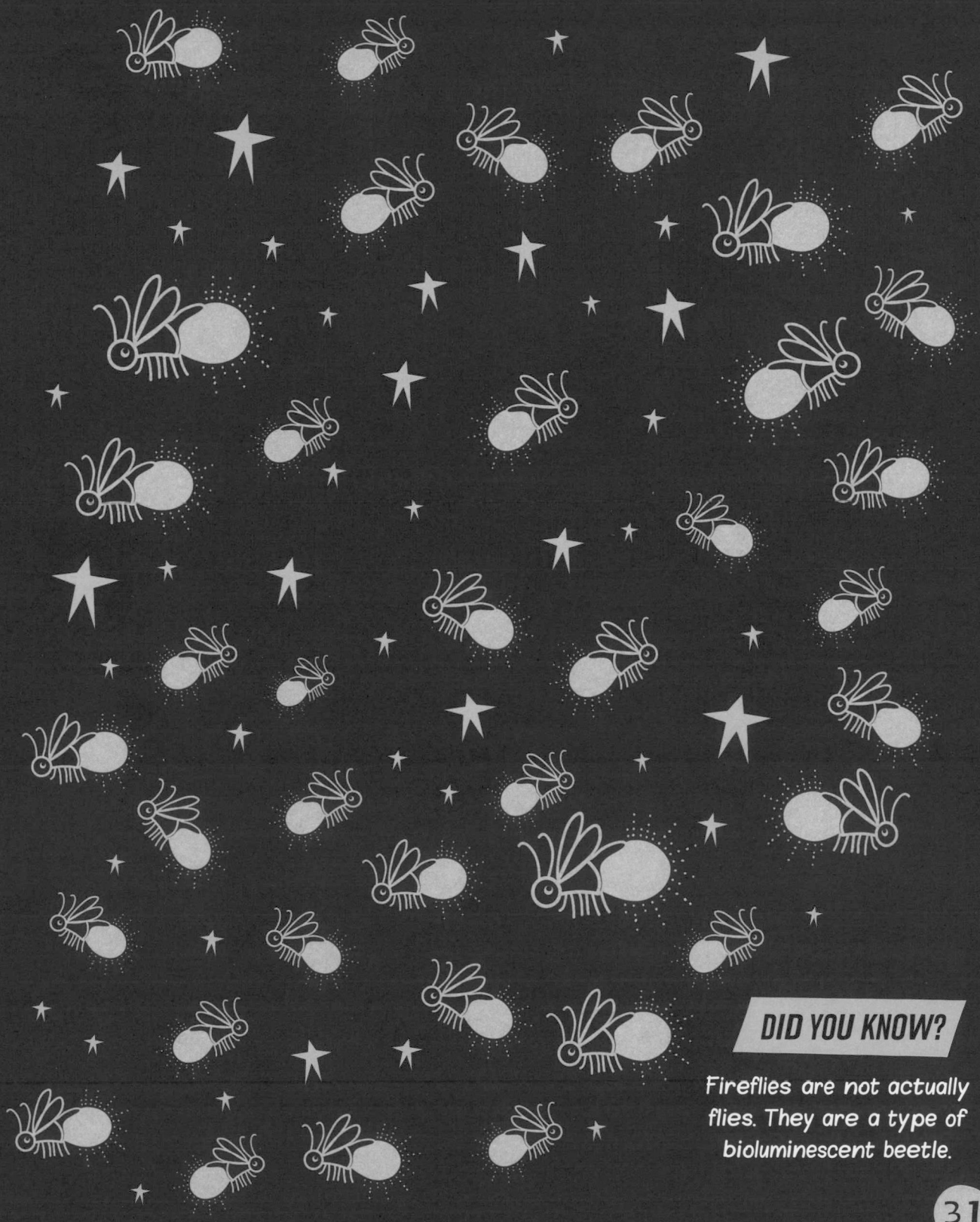

DID YOU KNOW?

Fireflies are not actually flies. They are a type of bioluminescent beetle.

What is out of place in this scene?

Can you work out the sequence that these shells follow?
Fill in the blank shells with the right pattern.

Is there an odd or even number of deer below?
Count them and find out!

Busy beehive word search!
Find all of these words in the grid below.

HIVE
HONEY
QUEEN
COLONY
BUZZ

FLOWER
POLLEN
SWARM
WAX
INSECT

A
F M
H R G
G A E V
K W V C D
Q S I B Q F
D B H Z Z U L
B U Z Z B H E O
C O L O N Y O E W
W Q U E F D B N N E
A N E L L O P J E K R
X B I N S E C T Z Y U Q

Can you find the row that matches the silhouette?

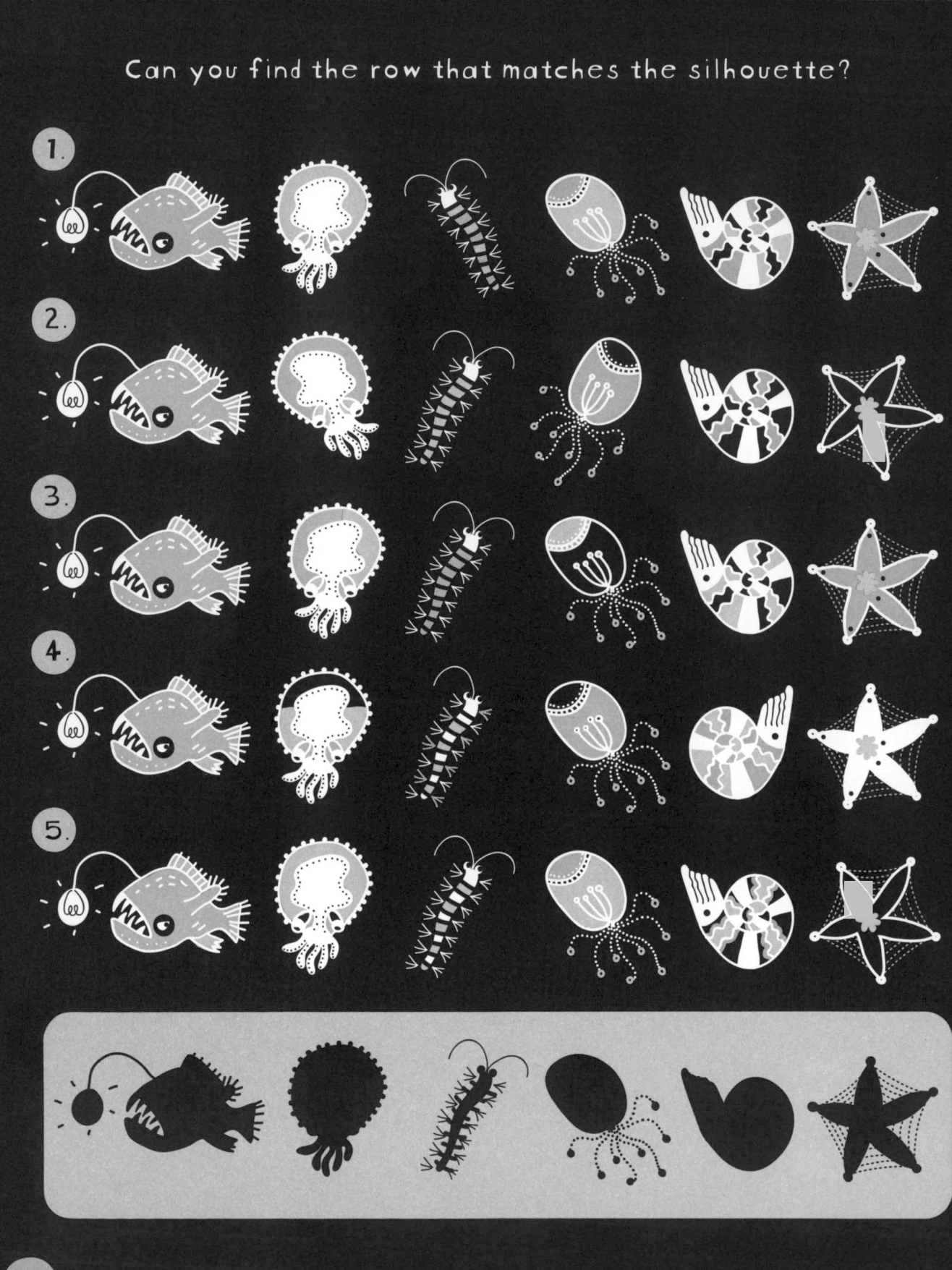

Dinner time! Who's eating what?

Add stripes to the bees so that each row (across, down, and diagonal) adds up to 15 stripes.

Can you complete this picture grid? Fill in all of the boxes with one of the four pictures. Every column, row, and four-square block must contain one of each.

QUICK QUIZ!

1. Why do elephants have big ears?

a) To help them fly b) To keep the sun out of their eyes

c) To keep them cool d) To keep their glasses on

2. How old is the world's oldest living tree?

a) 95 years old b) 950 years old

c) 9,550 years old d) 95,550 years old

3. The largest rainforest on Earth is called?

a) eBay b) The Congo c) The Amazon d) Agnes

4. The highest mountain peak on Earth is on which of these?

a) Mount Everest b) Mountain Big Rock

c) Mount Etna d) Mount Ain

5. The biggest pig ever weighed more than 2,500 pounds and was 9 feet long! What was his name?

a) Giant Geoff b) Big Bill

c) Huge Henry d) Biggus Piggus

Only two of these birds have identical patterns.
Can you spot them?

Which monkey gets back to the baby monkey first?
Work out the sums. The monkey with the highest total wins!
Use a separate piece of paper if you need to.

Can you find these squares in the picture below?

Can you break this code to reveal the picture? Color in each of the squares in this list to see what is hidden.

A - 10, 11, 12, 13
B - 9, 14
C - 8, 15
D - 3, 4, 5, 6, 7, 11, 15
E - 2, 15
F - 1, 2, 3, 4, 5, 6, 7, 8, 15
G - 9, 13, 14
H - 10, 11, 12
I - 2, 9, 13
J - 2, 8, 13
K - 2, 8, 14
L - 2, 7, 14
M - 2, 6, 9, 15
N - 2, 5, 10, 15
O - 2, 4, 10, 15
P - 2, 3, 4, 5, 6, 7, 8, 9, 10, 15
Q - 2, 3, 15
R - 4, 5, 14
S - 6, 7, 8, 9, 10, 11, 12, 13, 14
T - 8, 11
U - 8, 11
V - 8, 11

	1	2	3	4	5	6	7	8	9	10	11	12	13	14	15	16	17
A																	
B																	
C																	
D																	
E																	
F																	
G																	
H																	
I																	
J																	
K																	
L																	
M																	
N																	
O																	
P																	
Q																	
R																	
S																	
T																	
U																	
V																	

Answers

Page 3
COSTA RICA

Page 4
EVEN = 7
ODD = 9
Carly wins!

Page 6

Page 8

Page 10

F	Y	D	I	V	E	R	S	V	M	S	H	H	S	H	K
I	S	X	K	T	U	R	T	P	E	U	S	X	T	M	I
S	S	Q	S	P	E	C	I	E	S	I	L	U	U	A	R
D	T	O	U	W	R	H	M	K	F	D	H	S	R	X	O
H	A	L	R	I	Q	J	H	A	L	G	A	E	T	M	P
P	R	F	E	V	D	E	B	L	M	A	X	A	L	J	I
L	F	E	F	D	S	L	E	N	H	X	H	W	E	H	C
K	I	E	F	X	L	L	L	A	R	O	C	E	M	S	A
E	S	R	B	E	G	Y	X	P	O	C	X	E	V	H	L
Y	H	P	H	S	K	F	M	C	R	T	X	D	H	A	M
F	D	S	L	O	W	I	N	K	L	O	U	Q	W	R	A
B	U	B	B	L	E	S	X	D	X	P	V	X	U	K	R
Q	L	G	X	J	F	H	N	X	M	U	K	E	L	P	C
G	R	O	C	E	A	N	S	H	E	S	K	L	E	S	M
J	A	L	S	E	A	W	R	E	F	L	L	E	H	K	P
K	B	A	D	E	E	P	S	E	A	X	M	B	A	R	C

Page 11

Page 12

Page 13

Page 16

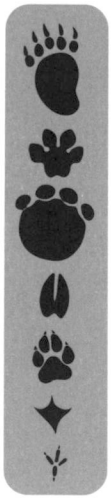

Page 17

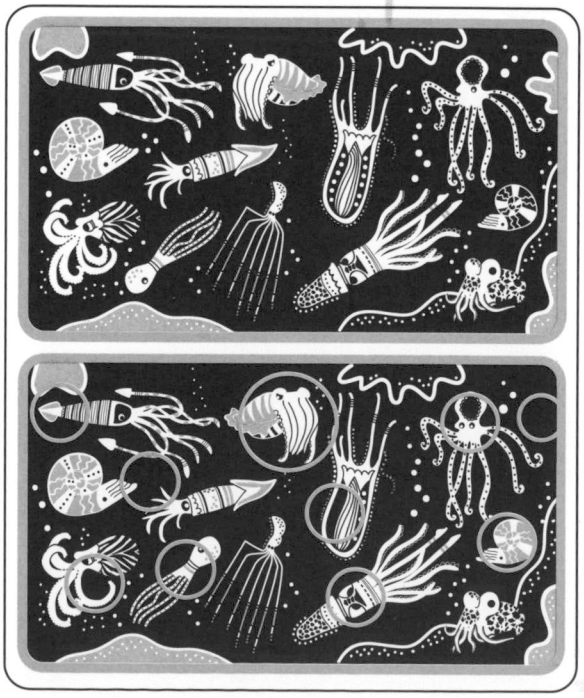

Page 15 - 1. True
2. False
3. True
4. False
5. True
6. False
(They take two!)

Page 18

Page 20

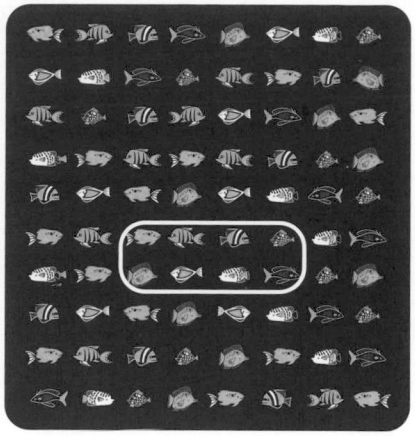

Page 22

Page 26

Page 27

Pages 28-29

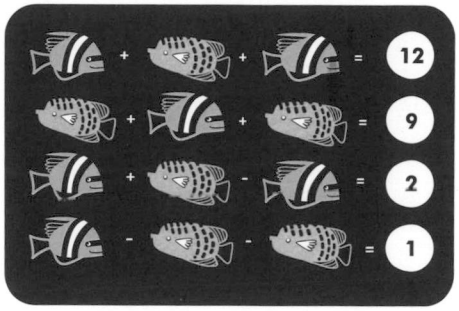

Page 31 - There are more stars.

Page 30

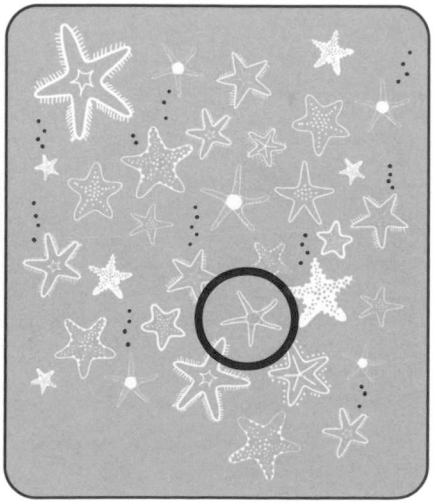

Page 32

Page 33

Page 34

EVEN
There are
14 deer.

Page 35

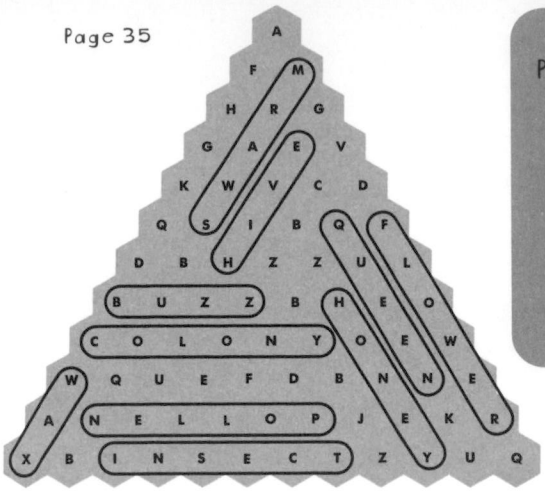

Page 40

1. c
2. c
3. c
4. a
5. b

Page 41

Page 36 - Row 3

Page 37

1. C 2. A 3. B

Page 42

A = 116 B = 125

B reaches the baby first.

Page 43

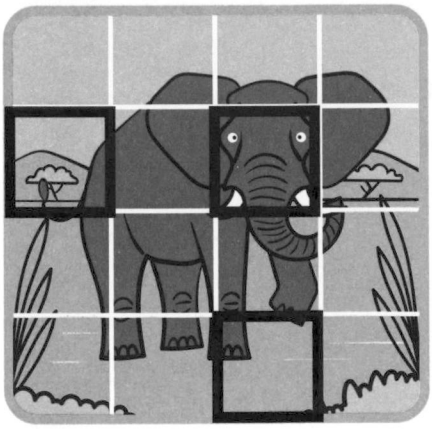

Page 38

Page 39

Pages 44-45

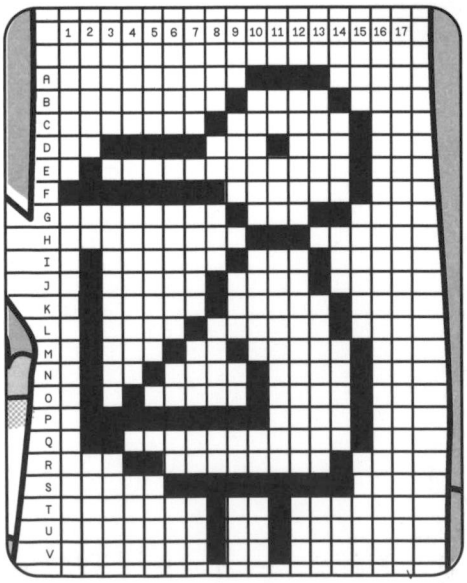